UNDERSTANDING SYSTEMS

It is important to be prepared for the transition from school to work.
Understanding systems is a skill that will help you to stand out.

THE LEARNING-A-LIVING LIBRARY

High Performance Through
UNDERSTANDING SYSTEMS

Bruce McGlothlin

THE ROSEN PUBLISHING GROUP, INC.
NEW YORK

Published in 1996 by The Rosen Publishing Group, Inc.
29 East 21st Street, New York, NY 10010

Copyright 1996 by The Rosen Publishing Group, Inc.

All rights reserved. No part of this book may be reproduced in any form without permission in writing from the publisher, except by a reviewer.

Library of Congress Cataloging-in-Publication Data

McGlothlin, Bruce.
    High performance through understanding systems / Bruce McGlothlin.
      p. cm. — (The Learning-a-living library)
    Includes bibliographical references and index.
    Summary: Discusses systems theory and how students can apply it to daily life and to career planning.
    ISBN 0-8239-2210-3
    1. Systems theory—Study and teaching—Juvenile literature.
[1. Systems theory. 2. Vocational guidance.] I. Title.
II. Series.
Q295.M4   1996
003—dc20
                                                  96-4166
                                                     CIP
                                                      AC

Contents

	Introduction	6
1)	What Is a System?	11
2)	What Is Systems Thinking?	17
3)	Systems at School	27
4)	Systems on the Job	33
5)	Systems Thinking and Your Career Path	39
	Glossary	58
	Organizations	60
	For Further Reading	61
	Index	63

Introduction

BRENT WAS FED UP WITH HIS JOB. HE WAS TIRED of working part time at a restaurant, peeling potatoes, shredding them into french fries, and cooking them in the deep fryer. These dull chores had absolutely nothing to do with his career goals. Brent wanted to get a job in agriculture once he graduated from high school. He loved working with plants and vegetables, and hoped one day to buy and run his own farm.

Since Brent lived in the city, there were no jobs nearby in the agricultural field. Because he thought that his current job was unrelated to his goal, Brent became restless. He started showing up late for work. His mind began to wander from his tasks, often causing him to make silly mistakes. Brent was so miserable that he decided to quit his job as soon as he got a chance to talk to the manager.

Brent did get an opportunity to see the manager, Maria, the next day. But before he had a chance to speak she asked him to take on an important

At any job, you are part of a larger chain of events.

responsibility on Saturday. "I usually get here at seven to receive the produce shipment on Saturday mornings," Maria explained, "but I'm going out of town for the weekend. Can you be here when the produce is delivered? I'll give you the list of items and the quantities we need, and you just check off the list with the delivery man." Brent was so pleased by the offer to do a different and more important task that he forgot about quitting.

Brent dragged himself out of bed at 6:15 A.M. on Saturday and made it to the restaurant by 7:00 A.M. The produce truck pulled up. As he watched the crates of vegetables and fruits being unloaded, Brent suddenly realized that all the produce originally came from a farm—perhaps like the farm he wanted to run someday. He had never before made the connection between the potatoes he peeled and the farmer who had grown them. Brent began to ask the delivery man questions about where the produce came from. He found out that the man worked for a distributor who bought produce from farms all over the state. Brent realized that he was part of a chain of events in the "life of a potato." He realized that he wasn't so far removed from his career goals after all. He understood now that as part of the food-service industry he was indirectly part of the agriculture business as well. All of a sudden, his job seemed more interesting and more relevant to his career goals.

Brent's attitude at work changed. He enjoyed working with the produce so much that he asked Maria if he could receive the shipment from now on. She was surprised and impressed. Soon, Brent took on the task of placing the order. He also took more pride in his own task of making the french fries, because he saw it as part of a larger system. His hard work and improved attitude paid off. In a year, he went from french fry maker to assistant manager.

By learning more about how the agriculture system worked, and his own role within it, Brent discovered the usefulness of systems thinking. You, like Brent, can become a systems thinker. You can understand how various systems, both on the job and at school, operate and interact with each other. You can modify or create systems to save your employer time and money and give yourself opportunities to develop and grow with the company.

This book explores the many systems that surround you every day and the ones that directly influence or involve you. It surveys the underlying concepts of systems thinking and shows how to apply them to improve and create your own systems in school and at work. Finally, it explains how systems thinking and other related skills can help you devise a career path and achieve your career goals.

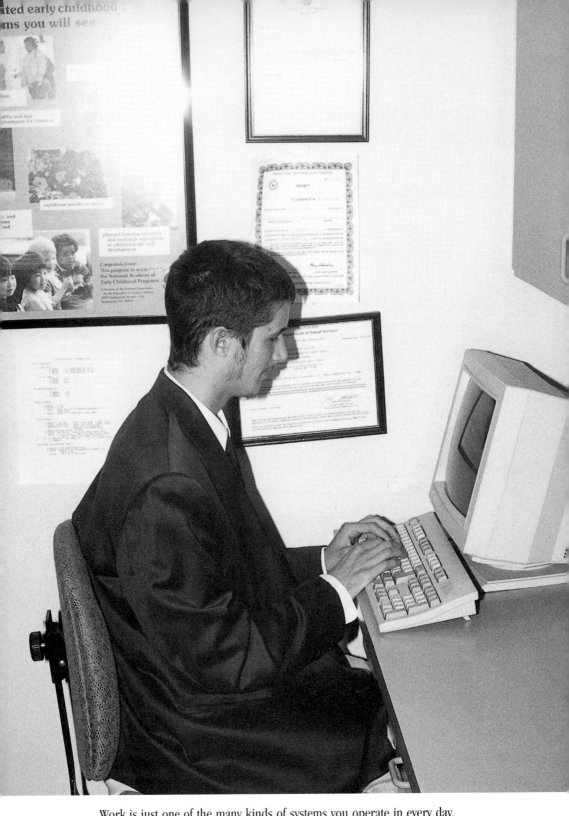

Work is just one of the many kinds of systems you operate in every day.

What Is a System?

A SYSTEM IS ANY COMBINATION OF ELEMENTS that operate together and form a whole. Systems may be biological, physical, political, social, or economic. You encounter and participate in different types of systems every day. For example, you are a participant in your school system. You may use your city's transportation system. When you buy something from a store, you are participating in the economic system that keeps our country running.

It can be useful to think in terms of systems as you move from school to the world of work. The most important types of systems to think about as you make this transition are social, organizational, and technological systems. But even more basic are the three types of systems you operate in almost every day: family systems, school systems, and job systems.

Family Systems
Family members are individuals with their own

Setting the table is an example of a chore that may be assigned to younger family members.

needs, desires, and goals. But these individuals must learn to live together as a family system, which has its own needs, desires, and goals. The family is the first system to which we are exposed, and the first system in which we participate. Family members work together as a system to solve problems, accomplish tasks, and set goals. Chores are a way of delegating tasks within a family system. If nobody bought groceries, the family would not eat. If nobody set the table, family members would not have plates or utensils with which to eat. You probably have your own role within the family system that is part of the larger workings of your family.

School Systems

In school, your role is to attend classes and study. Teachers, cafeteria workers, maintenance workers, counselors, and secretaries also have roles to play in the school system. Many subsystems—small systems operating within a larger system—are at work in a school. For example, systems such as grading and budgeting operate within the larger school system. Even subsystems that may not directly involve you still affect your role as a member of the school system in some way. Like family systems, school systems have rules and regulations to help them function effectively.

Job Systems

Like schools, most businesses rely on systems to keep everything running smoothly. Systems are an effective way for companies to reach their proposed goals or deadlines. At a restaurant, for example, each worker has a specific job to do. To achieve the goal of providing good food and fast service to the customer, every member of the restaurant staff must do his or her specific job. If one member fails to perform his or her task, the entire system is in danger of failing. And as a result of such individual

When completing a task at work, keep in mind the larger goal, such as making products more accessible to customers.

failures, the restaurant's larger goals may not be achieved.

Job systems are usually designed to save money and time so that the employer can produce as much as possible for the lowest possible cost. Specific tasks within the system are always designed with larger goals in mind. It will benefit you in your own job to think about how you fit into the larger system. By becoming an efficient systems thinker, you will have a better chance of receiving raises and promotions.

For example, if your weekend job involves stocking shelves at the supermarket, it helps to know how your job fits into the larger goals of the business. The more efficiently you perform your job, the more products are available for customers to purchase. And the more purchases customers make, the more money your store will make. Such increases in company income often lead to bonuses or raises for hard-working employees. Realizing how important you are to the success of the company will give you pride in what you do.

These are just a few examples of the systems that are woven into your daily life. While there are many other systems all around you, school systems and job systems are probably the most important to you right now. But now that we know what systems are, what can we do with them?

Questions to Ask Yourself

You are surrounded every day by different types of systems. Identifying these systems is the first step in becoming a "systems thinker." 1) What is a system? 2) What are some examples of systems? 3) What kinds of systems operate around or directly involve you? What is your role in them?

What Is Systems Thinking?

NOW THAT YOU HAVE SEEN THE MANY SYSTEMS that surround and influence everyday life, you must determine how you fit into them. You can ignore the systems around you, and let them continue to affect you without your knowledge. Or you can learn more about these systems and how they operate in order to improve them—or perhaps even create your own. When you use your knowledge of systems to detect problems and alter parts of the system to correct those problems, you are "systems thinking."

Key Elements of Systems Thinking

It isn't difficult to become a "systems thinker." All you need to do is develop a few important skills. The key elements of mastering systems thinking are:

- Understanding systems, their parts, how they function, and how to operate effectively within them
- Monitoring and adjusting performance within a system
- Improving or designing systems

Store owners often offer discounts and sales in the hope that customers will buy more.

Mastering these three skills will make you stand out as someone who can see the "big picture" and be flexible and effective in making changes.

The Underlying Concepts of Systems Thinking
Understanding systems and systems thinking allows you to see the relationships between people and processes. How do the elements of a system work together? Once you understand this, you will be able to see changes in patterns, and eventually you'll be able to predict how certain changes will affect a system. A movie theater manager, for example, knows that the first night a movie is shown is usually very busy. She knows that she needs more ushers and ticket-takers on duty that night, and that the concession stand should pop extra popcorn. Because she understands the relationship between how recently a movie has been released and how many people will attend, she is able to predict changes and adjust the system accordingly.

There are other key concepts that play a part in systems thinking.

Dynamic Complexity. When you want to improve your system in some way (increase sales, for example), you usually make a change that you think will help. Dynamic complexity occurs when the change you make actually causes a negative effect in the system, rather than a positive one as you had hoped. Sometimes the negative effect, or problem, can show up in an entirely different part of the system. But more often than not, dynamic complexity produces exactly the opposite effect of what was intended within the same part of the system.

Here is an example of how dynamic complexity causes problems:

Cool Looks, a clothing store, sold about the same number of blue jeans every month. One day in September, Ron, the owner, decided that he wanted to increase their monthly sales of jeans. After talking over some ideas with his employees, Ron decided to run an ad in the local newspaper advertising Cool Looks' low prices. The advertisement appeared in the paper that month, and sure enough, in October they sold fifty more pairs than in September. Ron was very pleased.

Sales remained great all through October, but by the time November rolled around, Cool Looks didn't have enough jeans in the store for all the customers who wanted to buy them. Word got around that Cool Looks was out of jeans. When they finally did get a new supply, the customers were shopping elsewhere. As a result, Cool Looks had hundreds of jeans that they were unable to sell. And when Ron checked the sales for November, he found that they had sold fewer jeans than they had in September—before he had started advertising. The change he had made to increase sales actually caused sales to decrease two months later. The sales system experienced the damaging effects of dynamic complexity because of Ron's inability to foresee how his new advertisement would affect his supply of jeans.

Stocks and Flows. A stock is something that accumulates or builds up in a system. Stocks can be anything that gathers in a system, whether it's orders for products or the products themselves. Flows are the factors or changes in a system that cause the stock to increase or decrease.

At Cool Looks, jeans were the stock that collected in the store. Ron had hundreds of surplus jeans after his customers stopped coming to buy them. What was the flow (the reason that the jeans stock increased so much)? Ron's newspaper advertisement was the flow that caused the amount of jean stock to rise.

Reinforcing Processes and Positive Feedback Loops. When a change in the system continues to gradually improve some aspect of the system, a reinforcing process is operating. If that reinforcing process causes positive change, a positive feedback loop exists.

If sales at Cool Looks had continued to rise

month after month as a result of Ron's advertisement, the change would have been a reinforcing process. In this scenario, the increased sale of jeans would lead to greater and greater sales. Since the sales would continue to rise from October to November, to December, and so on, it would become a positive feedback loop. Each new month, the sales from the previous month would cause an increase in the sales, creating a positive feedback loop.

Balancing Processes and Negative Feedback Loops. If a process within the system acts to slow down other parts of the system, the action is called a balancing process. Since the effect of the process is negative and it decreases productivity, it causes a negative feedback loop.

This is what actually happened at Cool Looks. The process of ordering jeans did not happen fast enough to meet the increased demand. The shortage of jeans actually slowed down the positive effects of the advertisement. Therefore the ordering process was a balancing process. And because the effect of the advertisement was negative and sales decreased the next month, the entire process is a negative feedback loop.

Delay. Delay happens when the change that you

Sometimes, a marketing technique will have the effect of decreasing sales—the opposite of what was intended.

make in the system does not produce a positive or negative result right away.

When Ron placed the advertisement, his jeans sales increased the very next month. There was very little delay in the time it took for the store to show positive results. But there was a one-month delay before the sale of jeans started to fall. The negative change, a decrease in sales, did not occur immediately after Ron made a change in his system; it was delayed.

If you understand how these underlying concepts can affect a system, you will be able to make changes that cause positive effects and you will be able to avoid changes that lead to negative effects or slow your system down. Systems thinking can help you make changes that will benefit your business, your employer, and yourself.

Improving and Monitoring Systems

With any type of system, it helps to think about questions such as: How does the overall system work? What is its organizational structure? How does each person fit in? Do things run smoothly, or are problems constantly occurring? The answers to such questions alert you to changes that may be required. Often these changes must be small so that they do not disrupt the entire system.

Once changes have been made, it is important to know how they affected the system. Did they have a positive or negative effect? Did people handle the changes well? Did things run more smoothly after the changes were made? If not, why not?

Systems must be constantly monitored. Sometimes they stop working effectively, and an entirely new system must be developed. This can be a very challenging task. But now that you know some basic concepts of systems thinking, you are ready to change existing systems or create your own systems. In the following chapters we meet some young people who are using systems thinking to improve systems at school and work.

Questions to Ask Yourself
Understanding how systems operate will help you become more involved in their workings. Answer these questions to test your understanding of systems thinking. 1) What skills are involved in systems thinking? How can you learn such skills? 2) What is delay, and how does it affect systems? 3) Do you notice any problems within the systems in your life? What can you do to correct these problems?

Your school's grading system helps you, your parents, and your teachers to monitor your performance.

Systems at School

SCHOOL IS AN IMPORTANT PART OF YOUR LIFE right now. Succeeding at school can pave the way for future success. Understanding the systems involved at school can help you fine-tune your systems thinking skills—skills that you can then apply to your job and future career.

Grading is an example of a system at work in your school. Grades indicate how well you and other students are performing. The information provided by grades can be useful to students, parents, teachers, and administrators. College admissions officers, and even employers, may be interested in your academic performance to determine how well you would fit into their systems.

Teachers base their grading systems on elements such as homework, tests, research papers, and classroom behavior. Organizing yourself to meet a teacher's criteria for a certain grade is a way of operating effectively within a grading system. To succeed in the grading system, you must complete

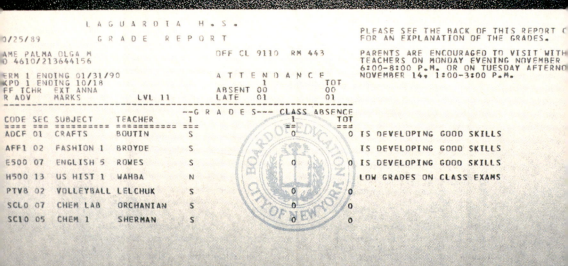

Completing assignments on time will have a positive effect on your performance in your school's grading system.

homework assignments effectively and on time, pay attention in class, and perform well on tests and other in-class assignments.

Improving Performance at School

Tracy was a consistent C student in English, but when she decided that she wanted to write for the school paper, she knew she would have to pull up her English grade. She talked to her English teacher about how to improve her performance. He suggested that she spend more time checking her papers for spelling mistakes and other careless errors. The next time she wrote a paper, Tracy gave herself an extra hour to check the spelling on the computer and print out a draft copy to proofread. She corrected a lot of mistakes, and her grade reflected the extra time and effort she put into the paper. Her grade in English went up to a B, and she made it onto the newspaper staff the following term. Tracy worked with her teacher to diagnose her problem, and she improved her performance. She learned how to operate more effectively within the grading system in order to achieve her goal of writing for the school paper.

Learning About Acquiring Funds

Carlos was a member of his school's service club. The club's goal was to create new projects within the school. Members had observed that the old concession stand at the football field was falling apart. The club decided to build a new concession stand.

Carlos and the other group members reviewed school and club procedures to determine how to accomplish their goal. They knew that they could not simply ask the school for money to build a new stand. They consulted the school principal, who agreed to act as their adviser. He suggested that they develop a written proposal about the new stand, its approximate cost, and how funds for construction would be raised.

With the help of a local architect and contractor,

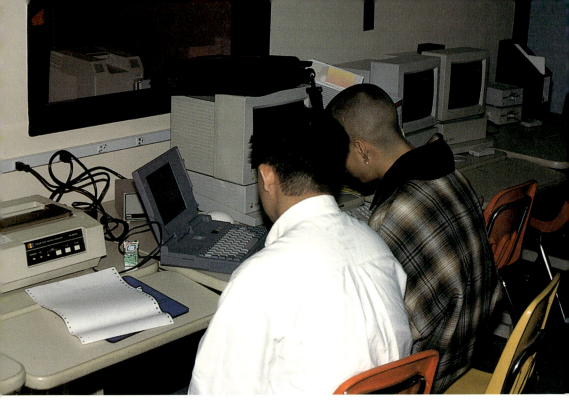

In working to accomplish a goal in a school project or activity, you might find it helpful to share tasks with others.

they developed a proposal. The principal presented it to the school board. The board agreed to organize a committee to study the proposal, and the club worked with the committee to devise a cost-effective plan. As a result, Carlos learned about the complicated system of budgeting money for school programs. He saw how the principal worked with the school board and how the school board had its own system for making decisions.

Designing Your Own System at School
Once you decide on a goal, you can create your own system to achieve that goal. You may want to raise money so that your choir can take trips and sing in

other cities. You will need to organize choir members to play different roles within the system. Some people may be involved in fundraising. Others may start to plan the tour itself. Still others may choose the songs that the choir will sing.

As the person in charge of the system, you need to monitor the performance of other choir members as well as your own. You are responsible for correcting mistakes and suggesting alternatives if parts of the system aren't working exactly as you had planned.

If you start learning your school's systems, you can begin to make changes in your part of those systems. You will not only improve your own performance but strengthen the greater system as well. And because you have developed your systems thinking skills at school, you will be able to apply what you have learned to your after-school or weekend job.

Questions to Ask Yourself
Your school is a complex system that affects your life almost everyday. You can use systems thinking to improve your performance at school. 1) What are some of the subsystems that comprise your school system? 2) Do you have any classes in which you are having trouble? What people in the system would be best to talk to for help? 3) How can systems thinking be applied to clubs and activities?

At your job, ask questions about how the company works so that you can better understand your own role.

Systems on the Job

REMEMBER BRENT FROM THE INTRODUCTION OF this book? He used systems thinking to turn around his attitude and his performance at work and to help him toward his ultimate career goal. A part-time or summer job is not just a way to earn extra money—it is also an opportunity to learn valuable workplace skills, including systems thinking. No matter where you work, you are part of a system, whether you work in a clothing store, coffee shop, a service station, or even in a home as a baby-sitter. Recognizing your role in a system can help you to better understand your own tasks as an employee. You may even find that you can devise systems to make your own job easier and more efficient. Or you may find that the system you work in could actually be improved.

The System at Your Job

Every business has an organizational system. Employees have specific responsibilities and are monitored by a supervisor. When you start a new job, observe the organizational system and determine your own role in it. Thinking in this way will help you to monitor your performance and identify problems before a supervisor has to speak to you about them. Viewing the larger system will give you an edge over other employees who may simply focus on their own specific tasks. You will be better able to identify possible problems and suggest changes.

You will need to concentrate on being alert and knowledgeable, but it will pay off as your employer sees your eagerness to understand the workings of the company. You'll also be able to work better with others when you realize how your interactions figure into the organizational system. Understanding what other people do will also give you exposure to other types of jobs. After observing what the company's accountant does, for example, you may decide that you're interested in that field yourself.

Remember Brent, who began to be involved in purchasing produce for his restaurant? He realized that, although he was told to order five pounds of lemons and limes each time he ordered produce, only half of the limes were used. This was because the key lime pie did not sell as well in the winter, so the cook did not use as many limes. Lemons, on the other hand, were used for many things, and the demand for them was steady. Brent realized how the change of season would affect the larger system. His boss was pleased when he suggested to her that they could save money by ordering fewer limes. Suggesting improvements in the system at work shows initiative and creative thinking.

Changing a System at Your Job
Yvette got a summer job with a company called Running Feet, Inc. The store sold shoes for sports and fitness. Many of the styles were popular with teenagers. Yvette's friends were envious of her job because of her employee discount. "I really like their shoes," her friend Danny said. "But no way can I spend that kind of money. And it's hard for me to save money, too."

Yvette started thinking. Her friend Danny was a potential customer, but his inability to save money was keeping him from making a purchase. What could she do? The store couldn't help him save money—or could it? Yvette realized that there was a solution. She asked her manager if he would be open to the idea of a layaway plan, which allows customers to pay a portion of the cost of an item every week until they have paid the full amount. That way, Danny could bring his money right to the store and wouldn't have to worry about saving it himself.

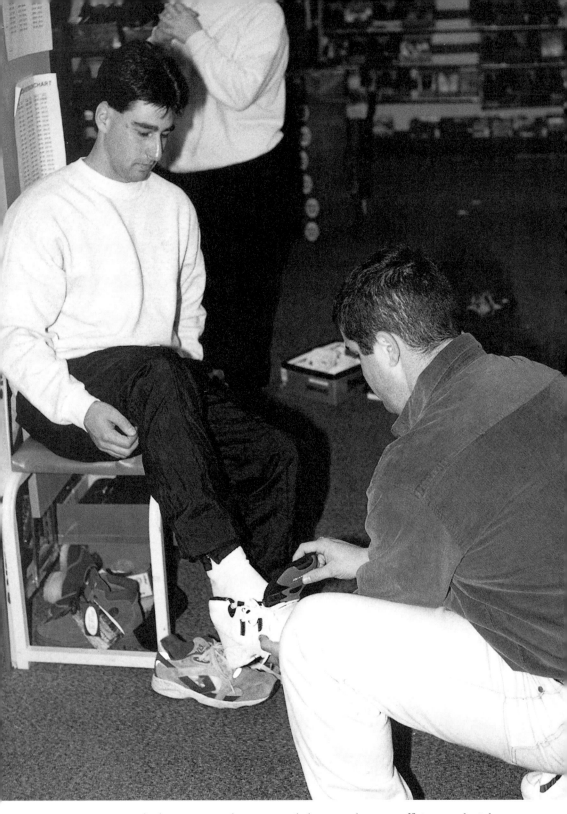
Using systems thinking to your advantage can help you to be more efficient on the job.

The manager was intrigued and told Yvette that he'd try the idea if she could design a system for the plan. She came up with ideas for advertising and designed forms to keep track of layaway purchases. She talked to the sales clerks about ways to make the system easy for them to use. She talked to the bookkeeper about how to account for layaway payments. She talked to her friends about whether the terms of the plan seemed reasonable to them as customers. She made sure that there was room in the back of the store to set aside layaway items. She considered potential problems—would the layaway plan be available for sale items or items that were low in stock? Should kids under a certain age need their parents' permission to leave money with the store?

By providing a new service, Yvette was able to improve on the existing sales system while creating a new one. The plan was a great success; the first week, dozens of students put down deposits on shoes. Yvette realized that she had a knack for sales. She applied for—and earned—a promotion to sales manager when an opening became available.

You can use systems thinking to your advantage, as Yvette did. You can locate potential problems in your business's system and make changes to avoid the problems before they begin. Your business will benefit, your boss will be happy, and best of all, you will have gained knowledge and experience that you can apply to your next level of work. Systems thinking can help you make the difficult transition from school and part-time jobs to your future career.

Questions to Ask Yourself
Using systems thinking can help you get promotions and raises at work. The following questions will help you understand how systems thinking can be applied to your job. 1) Are there any aspects of your job that could use improving? How could you change them for the better? 2) What habits should you develop to be a better systems thinker at work? 3) Why does systems thinking impress employers?

Systems Thinking and Your Career Path

As you have already read in earlier chapters, systems thinking is a useful skill to acquire now. Practicing it at school and in your job is especially important as you prepare to enter the workforce. It is not too early to start planning for your future. There are systems set up to help you choose a career path. Taking advantage of them is another way to practice your systems thinking skills. These skills are excellent preparation for your future career.

The workplace of the '90s is becoming a complicated and intimidating place for young people. To be successful, you need to present yourself positively to attract attention from potential employers. How do you do this? The ability to use systems thinking will make you stand out.

Looking Ahead

As mentioned earlier, the decisions you make while you are at school will influence your chances of achieving your career goals. If you take the time to

Talking to your school counselor can help you get ideas about your future career.

understand how your school's systems work and how they can help you, you will have more control over the path your life will take. Whether you hope to go to college or get a full-time job, there is no better time than now to start figuring out how to get there. By developing certain skills and making good choices now, you become more attractive to college admissions officers or potential employers.

Using Your School's Guidance System

Probably the best system your school has for helping you direct your career path is the guidance office. The people in that office have practical knowledge about the cause-and-effect relationship between what you do at school and the way you fit into the job world. They can tell you what courses you should take or what activities you should join to help you obtain a job in your chosen field.

The guidance department staff can also provide you with, or direct you to, books and other resources that will help you on your way. They often offer a variety of personality tests and personal interest questionnaires that can help you decide what fields might be best suited for you. They have books and catalogs that tell you not only what jobs or colleges may be best for you, but what you should do to get from here to there.

Your Classes and Your Career
The fact that you get good grades in all your courses doesn't mean that you will necessarily get the job you want. The courses that you choose to take can be an extremely important asset to obtaining your future job. You need to take courses that are relevant to your field of interest. By working with the guidance department, you can master the tricky system that exists between the school and job worlds.

Wallace, a sophomore in high school, had no idea what he wanted to do when he graduated. He decided to ask his guidance counselor for help. After talking for a while, Wallace and the counselor discovered that Wallace had an interest in cars and liked to build intricate models. A personality test later revealed that Wallace had a high capacity for mechanical tasks, perfect for a career in the automobile industry. Together, Wallace and his guidance counselor decided that he should enter the trade program and take courses that would teach him mechanics and other skills necessary for this field. By working with a member of the guidance department, Wallace was able to choose a career and take the first steps toward achieving his goal.

Computer Systems
One of the most important and influential kinds of systems in today's society is the computer. An individual computer is a complex system in itself, with its various parts (keyboard, disk drive, monitor) working together to accomplish different tasks. With the addition of a modem and telephone lines, a personal computer becomes part of an even greater system, communicating information with other computers around the world.

Nowhere in society has the computer's impact been greater than in modern business. Computers have become almost essential to the success of every kind of business today. Large companies use computer systems to communicate information

Computer skills are vital in today's workplace.

within their offices. Small companies use computers to keep track of their sales and to project future market conditions. No matter what a company does or how large its staff is, it probably uses a computer system to improve its speed and efficiency.

With the advent of the Internet and e-mail technology, the computer has become an even more important tool in the international marketplace. As part of an enormous system, your computer can send information to and receive information from computers on the other side of the street or the other side of the world. Company employees can do research without ever leaving the office. Businesses can advertise and sell products over the Internet. Computer systems are truly making the world a smaller place.

If you focus on developing your computer skills now, you will be better prepared to work within the corporate systems of the workplace. Because computers are such a central part of the business world, companies are constantly looking for employees with good computer skills to fill their positions. Obtaining computer experience can give you an edge over other applicants when you are looking for a job. Employers will know that you are capable of learning their computer system and fitting into their larger company system.

One way you can get the computer training you will need to excel in the world of work is to take classes in school that teach computer skills. Sometimes schools offer courses specifically about computer science or programming, but if yours doesn't, look for classes that offer some hands-on computer work in their curriculum. Even if the class is not specifically about computers, just gaining some familiarity with computers is a good first step for you to take. Ask your school guidance counselor about computer or computer-related courses in your school or in your area.

Activities

As guidance counselors will tell you, school and community activities can be important pieces in your job puzzle. Employers and college admission departments check the activities you list to see if you have acquired skills that will benefit them. Your participation in a marching band, football team, or community service organization reveals important aspects of your personality to prospective employers. As with courses, guidance counselors can help you get involved in activities that correspond to your career goals.

Carlos in chapter 3, for example, may have had an interest in business or finance. In that case, his work with the school board and principal to

Participation in school activities can help you stand out to potential employers.

construct the concession stand would be an excellent indication to colleges or employers of his abilities to work within systems. They would understand that Carlos has creative abilities and strong teamwork skills, desirable traits to most employers.

To get a job, advance quickly, and receive promotions, young people need to use systems thinking. Employers want to hire young people who can create new and fresh ideas. Whenever the company grows, systems-oriented workers will move up the career ladder.

Skills to Develop Systems Thinking

From reading this book, you should already have a good idea of systems thinking and what it involves. By focusing on certain skills, you can develop your systems thinking skills even further. You might even be using some of these skills already. But they will become even more important as you enter the high performance workplace. Becoming familiar with these skills now, and incorporating them into your activities at school and work, will put you a step ahead.

Much depends on what a worker brings to the job. What types of basic thinking skills does a person need to develop a successful "systems thinking" approach? Let's take a closer look at some of the ways that workers can contribute to an organization.

Creative Thinking

Employers want to hire workers who are creative and can produce new ideas. Workable new ideas mean increased production and more profit for the organization. These are the goals of most businesses.

Everyone possesses a certain degree of creativity. Each person looks at situations in different ways. Most creative ideas depend on how you approach a task. Open-mindedness and flexibility are the keys to being more creative, especially in the workplace. It is important to focus on performing a job

Brainstorming is a process in which people work together to find new ideas and solutions.

efficiently and observing how individual jobs fit into the entire structure of the company. Ask yourself, can this job or others be done more efficiently? This is using creative thinking in the workplace.

Reasoning

Reasoning involves common sense and practical knowledge about the job and the organization. When workers have learned the essentials of the operation, they bring their own reasoning skills to the jobs they perform. New methods can be initiated based on common-sense principles. This may improve efficiency levels.

By using reasoning skills, workers can understand how different jobs interact. Do the present methods of performing a job make sense in the broader scope of the company? Perhaps a new way would be better.

Brainstorming

This is a process that involves a high degree of creativity, independent reasoning, and positive group interaction. Workers come together to develop new ideas about the way jobs can be done or to solve a particular problem.

In brainstorming, all ideas and opinions are put forth. The pros and cons of each idea are discussed, and the idea is either adopted or discarded. The better ideas are narrowed down to the best ideas. If the best ideas do not work, the better ideas may be put to the test. Still further revisions may be needed.

Brainstorming can provide positive group interaction, and it helps to build good attitudes toward the organization, as employees realize that their opinions are valued.

Mental Visualization

This technique is abstract in nature. It encourages broad thinking. It can be used to think ahead and visualize how a particular idea or even an entire organization should function.

Mental visualization means looking to the future

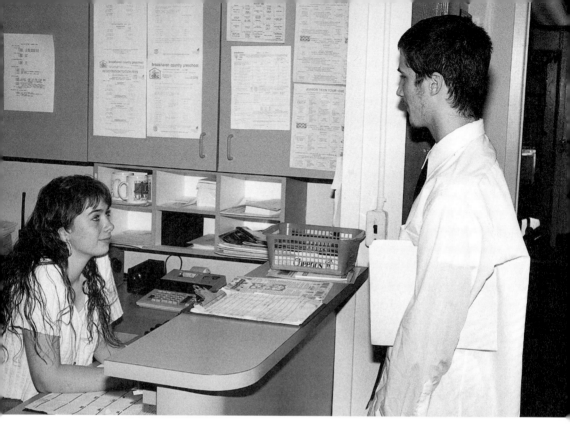
Arriving on time to interviews tells potential employers that you are aware of their need for punctual employees.

and imagining how new ideas would affect an organization. Possibilities are explored through imagination and creative ability rather than actually trying them out.

Employees who use mental visualization are one step ahead. They can predict the impact of changes in a system and point out potentially problematic effects. For employers, this foresight is extremely valuable.

Needs of Employers

Beyond their own basic job needs, young people

should observe the general needs of employers. This means being constantly aware of the current job market and possible trends that may be occurring.

Employers are always searching for knowledgeable and responsible employees who can perform well on the job. These employees are much like their employers in behavior, attitude, and values. Employers are more likely to hire people who display positive work traits and have positive goals for the future.

You can show an employer that you have positive work habits and goals on your first job interview. First, take the time to find out a little about the company where you will be interviewing. This kind of preparation will show the interviewer that you are responsible enough to prepare in advance. Also remember to dress neatly, arrive on time, and practice effective communication skills while interviewing. If you have the chance to discuss prior work or school experience, emphasize your role at the company in relation to the "big picture." Tell the interviewer how you were aware of your role, and how your contribution benefited the company.

For example, if your previous job was at a photo lab, you might say: "I took customers' orders, marking down the type of film and type of processing required. It was important to get this information right in order to avoid mistakes by the processing lab. I was also responsible for dealing with customer complaints and referring customers to the manager if their problem could not be solved by reprocessing their film. I think my job was important to the company because I was the link between customers and the lab and between customers and the manager. People get very concerned about their photos, so customer relations are important."

Systems thinking ideas gained in one organization can often be effectively applied to similar organizations in the future. Employers will value the perspective you can offer. They will also want you to be flexible as you learn their ways of doing things.

Understanding Limits

As workers develop their systems thinking processes, they realize that all systems have limits. Each particular system can go only so far.

Certain things within each system may never change. For example, raw materials may be purchased from one organization, even though it's less expensive to buy them from another. The company may have dealt with this supplier for years and have developed relationships that they are unwilling to break.

This can be very frustrating to those who try to improve the system. Some may continue to try to implement positive change; others will leave that system for another that offers more opportunities.

Each worker must decide if a particular system offers sufficient rewards and growth. Limits may exist that hinder future opportunities. It is important to realize that all systems have their limits, and you may have to cope with a system that cannot be modified or improved in the exact way you believe it should be.

Creating New Systems

Working within various systems can often lead to the creation of new ones. Understanding how different systems work together stimulates broader thinking about how various activities should be accomplished. Remember Yvette from chapter 4? She proposed the new layaway system for the shoe store where she worked. Creating a new system helped sales at the store and helped Yvette think about sales as a career.

Systems Thinking Skills in Action

Chris had always wanted to run his own video store. He had seen hundreds of videos and knew everything there was to know about the stars, the great directors, and the famous producers. He got a job at the local video store, Downtown Video, so that he could work with the movies he loved. Among his many responsibilities, Chris had to put the video tapes back on the shelves after they had been returned to the circulation desk.

One weekend, Chris and some of his co-workers noticed that it was taking far too long to shelve all the returned videos. Long lines would develop at the counter while the employees had their hands full of tapes. Customers would follow the employees around, waiting for them to shelve the new releases. Some customers even complained to the managers about the slow service.

Eventually, one of the managers asked Chris what he thought the problem was. Chris said it must be the system of shelving, which they had been using since the store first opened. At Chris's request, the manager scheduled an employee meeting to devise a solution to the problem as a group.

At the meeting, Chris explained the problem and suggested that they have a brainstorming session. As the employees mentally visualized the dilemma and used creative thinking to come up with suggestions, the manager wrote down all of the proposed ideas. After discussion, they narrowed the choice down to two ideas: that each employee work extra days so that there would be more people to shelve the videos, or that the sections be broken down into smaller, more specific categories so that the workers could shelve the videos faster.

Both proposed systems would solve the problem,

Systems thinking can help you to successfully design your own system.

but the manager pointed out that they didn't have much money in their budget for extra payroll. So they decided to try the system Chris proposed, to break down the current categories into smaller, specific sections. They asked Chris if he would be willing to organize the project. He happily accepted, and within months the store had a new system of organization and the customers stopped complaining.

A few months later, a managerial position opened at another Downtown Video location. Chris applied for the job. Based on the recommendation from his manager, Chris became the new manager. And after he accumulated five years of experience and pay, he bought his own store in the Downtown franchise with the help of a bank loan. Thanks to his initiative and his application of systems thinking, Chris was able to go from employee to store owner in just a few years. Systems thinking helped Chris achieve his career goals.

Chris was able to travel rapidly along his career path because of systems thinking. It all started with taking the time to understand how his system worked. After he was familiar with the operations of his system, it was easy for him to locate problems and decide what change to make in order to improve the situation. Chris also used his creative thinking and other abilities to impress his employers by devising and implementing a new system. Finally, he arrived at his career goal.

You can use systems thinking to improve the systems you are currently involved in and to progress toward your career goal. Whether you want to go to college or enter the working world, systems thinking can help you get from here to there. You can see all of the systems that surround you and understand how they affect your life. And because you know the underlying elements of systems thinking, you are better equipped to improve and create systems of your own. Once you master systems thinking at school and on the job, you will be able to set your career path and eventually achieve whatever career goal you choose. Put systems thinking to work for you!

Questions to Ask Yourself

Pretty soon, you will have to start thinking about your future career. Systems thinking can help you achieve your goals. 1) Where in your school system can you go for valuable advice on your career path? 2) What activities and classes are you involved in that will help you achieve your goals? Are there others that you can join? 3) What are some of the basic systems thinking skills? Which do you possess? Which do you need to work on?

Glossary

attitudes Ways that people consider other people, places, things, and events.

balancing process When a change in a system slows down other parts of the system.

brainstorming Method of generating new thoughts and ideas to solve problems.

cause-and-effect A relationship between an action and its resulting reaction.

change Adopting a way of doing tasks that is different from the present method.

cooperation Working successfully with others to accomplish goals.

creativity Ability to generate new ideas.

dedication A strong positive attitude toward accomplishing a goal.

delay In systems thinking, when a change in a system does not produce an immediate result.

dynamic complexity Business term meaning that a logical action produces an unexpected negative result.

goal Event toward which people work.

limits Final extent to which systems can operate.

management High-level supervisors of a company or organization.

mental visualization Thinking how an idea or situation will be in the future.

negative feedback loop In systems thinking, when a change in a system unexpectedly has a negative result.

organizational skills Abilities related to successful planning and organizing of time and events.

positive feedback loop In systems thinking, when a change in a system continues to result in positive change.

promotion Advancement to a higher position in a company.

reasoning Method of analyzing and solving a problem based on logic and common sense.

reinforcing process A process used to build on the positive result of a change.

rewards Positive recognition for accomplishing a goal.

stocks and flows Accumulation of products and how they are regulated.

system A combination of elements that operate together and form a whole, often in order to achieve a goal.

systems thinking Looking broadly at an organization and using creative skills to solve problems.

Organizations

Sources for Further Information on Jobs and Careers:

Academy of Administrative Management
550 West Jackson Boulevard
Chicago, IL 60661

Administrative Management Society
4622 Street Road
Trevose, PA 19047

American Society of Association Executives
1575 I Street NW
Washington, DC 20005

American Society for Training and Development
1630 Duke Street
Alexandria, VA 22313

For Further Reading

Bloch, Deborah Perlmutter. *How to Get a Good Job and Keep It*. Lincolnwood, IL: VGM, 1993.

Gilbert, Sara. *Go For It: Get Organized*. New York: Morrow Junior Books, 1990.

McFarland, Rhoda. *The World of Work*. New York: Rosen Publishing Group, 1993.

Phifer, Paul. *Career Planning Q's and A's: A Handbook for Students, Parents, and Professionals*. Chicago: Ferguson, 1990.

Templeton, Mary Ellen. *Help! My Job Interview Is Tomorrow!: How to Use the Library to Research an Employer*. New York: Neal-Schuman Publishers, 1991.

Challenging Reading

Boulding, Kenneth Ewart. *The World as a Total System*. Beverly Hills, CA: Sage Publications, 1985.

Bowler, T. Downing. *General Systems Thinking: Its Scope and Applicability*. New York: North Holland, 1981.

Career Sourcebook 1: A Guide to Career Planning and Job Hunting. Washington, DC: Edison Electric Institute, 1988.

Clifton, H.D., and Sutcliffe, A.G. *Business Information Systems*. New York: Prentice Hall, 1994.

Weinberg, Gerald M. *An Introduction to General Systems Thinking*. New York: Wiley, 1975.

Index

A
activities, 45–46
agriculture, 6–9

B
balancing processes, 22
brainstorming, 49, 54
budgeting, 13, 30

C
career path, 9
    systems thinking and, 39–57
change
    negative, 23
    positive, 21–22
common sense, 48–49
community service, 45
computer systems, 42–45
courses, choice of, 41–42
creative thinking, 47–48, 49, 50, 56

D
delay, 22–23
dynamic complexity, 19–21

E
e-mail, 44

F
flexibility, 48
flows, 21
food-service industry, 8–9

G
goals, 12
    career, 9, 57
    unmet, 14–15
group interaction, 49

I
Internet, 44

J
job interview, 51–52

L
layaway plan, 35–37
limits, understanding, 52–53

M
mental visualization, 49–50

N
negative effect, 19–20, 21, 22–23, 24
negative feedback loop, 22

P
performance
   improving, 28–29
   monitoring, 31, 34
personality tests, 41, 42
positive feedback loop, 21–22

R
reasoning, 48–49
reinforcing process, 21–22
role, recognizing, 33

S
skills
   computer, 42–45
   to develop systems thinking, 17, 47, 53–57
   systems thinking, 39
stocks, 21
subsystems, 13
systems
   changing, 35–38
   designing, 17, 30–31, 33, 37, 53
   family, 11–13
   fitting into, 15, 17
   grading, 13, 27–29
   guidance, 40–42, 45
   improving, 17, 24–25, 33, 35–38
   job, 11, 13–15, 33–38
   monitoring, 17, 24–25
   organizational, 11, 33–34
   school, 11, 13, 27–31
   social, 11
   technological, 11
   understanding, 17, 56
systems thinking
   concepts of, 19–24
   elements of, 17–19
   usefulness of, 9, 24

T
tasks
   completing, 13–15
   delegating, 12

About the Author
Bruce McGlothlin is a school psychologist and counselor in Pittsburgh, Pennsylvania. He holds graduate degrees in school psychology and counseling. He is the author of several books for young adults including: *Traveling Light, Great Grooming for Guys, Search and Succeed,* and *Careers Inside the World of Sports and Entertainment.* Bruce and his wife, Judi, are the parents of two teenage children, Michael and Molly.

Photos
Cover by Kim Sonsky. All other photos by Kim Sonsky and Matthew Baumann.

Layout and Design
Kim Sonsky